Awakening

Bridgette Mclauchlin

Presentation by *BookLeaf Publishing*

Web: www.bookleafpub.com

E-mail: info@bookleafpub.com

ISBN: 9789357212786

First edition 2023

Dedicated to the ones who have loved me at my darkest;

you are the reason I survive the hell inside my mind.

ACKNOWLEDGEMENT

First, I want to say thank you to the ones reading this. Thank you for taking a chance on me; I hope it was worth it. If you relate to anything in this book, I want to say I'm so sorry, but I also want you to know that I see you, and your feelings and experiences are real and valid. Don't ever give up- it may be dark now, but the sun will rise again, and you will rise with it. If you're going through something or you've been through something, I pray that you find peace and healing.

Secondly, thank you to my family, and a special thank you to my husband, who has been my biggest supporter since the day we met. I thank God for you every day, and I love you so much more than words could say!

Thank you to my friends and extended family. To my best friends who are always hyping me up, and are always there whether it's good or bad times. I could never express my gratitude enough for your support and unconditional love.

Lastly, a special thank you to Caroline for notifying me about this opportunity in the first place. You are such a fantastic woman and an extraordinary friend. May this be the beginning of the many goals we accomplish both individually and as the soul sisters we are.

PREFACE

I can't help but think
That I unscrewed the lid
Of my subconscious
And allowed all the pain that was hidden
To escape.

And I can't put it back in,
Now that it's all out in the open.
A suitcase of a subconscious,
That will never zip closed again.

Candlelight

As wax drips beneath fire, they dance
And so begins this twisted romance.
A waltz of back and forth
Give and take
A constant battle
Between love and hate.

Throughout hell she loves him the same
Forever he will be her flame
Cradled underneath his thumb
She becomes gullible
And at the snap of his fingers
She starts to crumble.

She melts at his blazing touch,
But oh, how she loves him so much!
And he burns and burns her up,
Until she's given him every last drop.

Boy Was I A Fool

Boy, was I a fool
To think the butterflies
Were simply nerves
When it was a warning for
The pain I wouldn't deserve.

Boy, was I fool
To believe one minute
Your love was true
And look away from the shadows
peeking through your eyes of blue.

Boy, was I a fool
To fall for the games
You'd play
With my head and my heart
Every day.

Boy, was I fool
To allow myself to deteriorate
At the hands
Of an abuser who believed
he was a man.

Boy, was I fool
To give you the intimate
Parts of me
Watching you use and discard them
As you please.

Boy, was I a fool
To believe the words you'd say
When you told me I was
Beautiful
Ugly
Precious
Worthless
Loved
Hated

Boy, was I a fool
To fall in love with you.

Your Love

Your love was like the ocean
Unknowing but enticing
Comfortingly cool when the sun
Burned and left me raging hot.

Your hands gentle
Washing over me
Like water lapping and reaching for my feet
Pulling me in more and more.
From feet to ankles,
Ankles to knees,
Knees to hips,
To waist,
Until I'm submerged completely.

Your love was like the ocean,
A paradise to spend the rest of my days.
Giggling and splashing,
Laying next to
The sound that soothes me
As the sun sinks under the horizon.

Your love is like the ocean
Deep
Dark and haunting

Raging, unforgiving
Filled with secrets
And dangerous, unknown creatures
Grasping at limbs hungrily
Angry and mercilessly,
Pulling down.

Scarlet

Fingers dance along her skin
Tracing a path of unholiness
But she forgets her sin
When he wraps her in such bliss.

Her innocence fled
Along with her cares
When he lays her in his bed
And their hands travel everywhere.

Sweat, fire, lips,
All things burn
Grab, squeeze, grip,
The pull on her heart is firm.

He left a scarlet letter
Sewn into her chest
She thought she knew better,
But he had her at her best.

Her mouth draws his name,
But she is not who calls him.
He leaves her in ashes from his flame,
As his lust for her begins to dim.

The Roommate in Apt. 21

She stands, clothed in darkness,
And paces the walls in my mind.
Her room is always hollow and empty,
So she's never hard to find.

She makes herself at home quickly,
She's active and careless,
Like a tornado in a glass house.
And she tells me I'm pathetic and worthless.

I should just off myself,
She already has a plan in place.
"JUST SWALLOW THE DAMN PILLS!" She
screams,
With black tears flowing down her face.

She's never leaving,
No matter how many times I throw her out.
Days later I find her in her room,
Toying with my doubts.

My fears, my past, she knows everything.
There's no escape from her.
She holds me close as I mourn,
Over my happiness she murders.

I can't let anyone in,
I can't let them see,
Because she might hurt them, too.
She's territorial over me.

She's chaotic and unpredictable.
People say she's crazy.
She's a disease that won't leave,
She's permanently a part of me.

Until my last day on Earth,
Until my final breath,
Her name is Depression,
And she's all I'll have left.

Fantasy

9

You put your hand
Around my throat
And I moaned.

Because I lust after death
Like a release
I can feel in my bones.

Silence is my Fortress

People always ask me
"Why are you so quiet?"
Because I can't be laughed at,
Or judged based off my words,
If the gates of my lips never open.
I can't be criticized for saying what I'm thinking,
If my thoughts are confined
To the tower of my mind.
"Why are you so quiet?"
The answer is simple, really.
Because as long as my mouth is shut,
I'm safe.

Death

I stared Death in the face
As he loomed in the corner of the room
Sometimes for years,
For days, or for mere hours.

I told him
It was okay,
To take away my loved ones
Even when it was not.

I've sat numbly In these rooms
And I've cried in these rooms.

And I've let go of hands
I would never hold again.

The Irony

12

There's a lesson I learned
That grief is much more than death.
You can mourn someone
Or something
Just as much in life.

And the teacher of this lesson,
The person who taught me this,
Walked away from me too,
Long before they were laid to rest.

Don't Ask Me

Until you have held your dreams
Quite literally in the palms of your hands
And cradled the remains of a life
You've wanted for so long
But could never have.

Until you have sat
Shaking and sobbing
As the blood that raced down your legs
Mixed with the tears flowing down your face
And the love of your life looked on
Helpless and afraid

Until you have pleaded and demanded
And bargained with God Himself,
Because the light that He has created in you
Was slowly dimming out
And you weren't ready
To lie among the ashes inside of your self doubt.

Don't ask me why I'm angry,
Or jealous or put off,
Don't ask me where I am in my faith.
Don't ask me why I suddenly begin to cry
Or why you haven't heard from me in days.

Because until you have clutched on
To everything you had ever wanted
And screamed for it not to leave you,
I don't think you would truly understand
Exactly what I've been through.

The Bitter Truth

15

No one
Is going to hold you
Through your grief.
Because it's not
Their memories
Or reminders
It's not their dreams
It's not their sorrow
Nor is it their loss.
It's yours.

Darling, how can they
Know the depths of
What you have lost
If they never understood
What you had
In the first place?

It All Hurts the Same

16

You can lose the people you love
To other things,
Not just death.

Conversations with God

17

I wonder if you talk to God about me
As you look down from heaven.
I wonder if you tell Him how proud you are.

Her.

I saw her;
The woman who
Danced beneath the flashing lights,
Because she wanted to,
Until she needed to,
In order to survive.

I saw her;
The woman who
Picked nicotine as her poison
Taking drags from a menthol
The cigarettes more comforting
Than the company she was keeping.

I saw her;
The woman who
Watched the liquor endlessly poor
Like raindrops in a hurricane
More and more and more.

I saw her;
The woman who
Peered at herself in a dirty mirror
Applying cheap makeup as her disguise
And painted on a smile
That never reached her eyes.

I saw her;
The woman who
Used to be me
But I am no longer
Her.

Brown Eyes

Brown eyes are just brown eyes,
Until you fall in love with someone with brown
eyes.
Gone are the shades of blue
Of oceans, and skies, and reckless love without a
clue.
Gone are the shades of green,
Of trees and grass, and simple love as it may
seem.

Instead, you see a steady flame,
And love as you know it is never the same.
They bore into you, with deep embers of
innocence,
Captivating you until it all seems to click.
They may seem dark, but don't let them fool
you,
There is love and longing waiting to show
through.

See, brown eyes aren't just brown eyes,
They're the eyes that hold you when you cry.
They're the eyes that long for you with passion
so deep,

They're powerful enough to put your anxiety to
sleep.
And once you've found those eyes that shake
you to the core,
You find yourself in love, and then you're done
for.

Foreign Land

I fell in love with you again
And I was comfortable
Because it was a place
I was familiar with.

I knew my way around
Every corner and crevice.
It was my resting place,
It was my solace.

But the unknown gnaws at me
Gently, but noticeably
Some things have changed.
The crevices are deeper
The corners are sharper
Both intimate and outlandish.

And it's strange-
Both frightening and fascinating,
How a person I knew my way around
A person I once called home
Became a foreign land,
Somewhere I've never been before.

I Once Loved Love

I once loved love so much,
But love didn't love me.
Love was a friend I thought I knew
But didn't know truly.

I loved love so much
I chased it like a dream
Inhaling it from my lips
And into my bloodstream.

I once loved love so much
I thought it was exhilarating
Like a shot of adrenaline
That left my heart incinerating.

I once loved love so much,
I sold myself short frequently
To every boy who took advantage
Of my vulnerability.

I once loved love so much,
I watched it leave
And I once loved love so much
That I never truly loved me.

I Am.

24

I am not crazy.
I am a woman
With a brain
That doesn't produce enough chemicals
To be considered normal.

I am not my pain
Nor am I the mistakes I made
That caused hurt to myself
And to those I loved the most
Even those I hadn't met yet.

I am not my trauma
Nor am I the one I was
When the darkness closed in
And I lost the ones
I wanted to hang on to.

I am not my physical being
Nor am I defined by the lines
Of stretch marks
That trace my stomach
My chest
And my thighs.

I am a laugh
So loud and belly-deep
Head back and eyes closed
Uncaring of who hears me.

I am the one
Diving head first
Into the cold, salty sea,
Despite the monsters that lurk underneath.

I am a smile
That admires the sky
When my Creator paints a beautiful sunset
Because He painted me before my very first cry.

I am a woman
Though in the dark at times
The sun comes up again
And with it I will rise.

I am strong

I am worthy

I am significant

And I am so, so beautiful.